Table of Contents

Introduction

Oatmeal Recipes:

Peanut Butter and Raspberry Jelly Stovetop Oatmeal

Spiced Pumpkin Stovetop Oatmeal with Pecans

Cheesy Mushroom Stovetop Oatmeal

Cherry Chocolate Almond Stovetop Oatmeal

Sriracha Soy Green Onions and Corn Stovetop Oatmeal

Copy-Cat Carrot Cake Stovetop Oatmeal

Creamy Coconut and Strawberry Stovetop Oatmeal

Nutty Cinnamon Blueberries and Peaches Stovetop Oatmeal

Creamy Mango Coconut Stovetop Oatmeal

Salted Caramel Apple Pie Stovetop Oatmeal

Cheesy Bacon Stovetop Oatmeal with Egg

Creamy Coconut Cafe Latte Overnight Oatmeal

Birthday Cake Overnight Oats

Strawberry Cheesecake-Inspired Overnight Oatmeal

Blueberry Overnight Oats

French Toast-Flavored Overnight Oats

Coco-Mango and Ginger Overnight Oats

Blueberry Muffin-Tasting Overnight Oats

Fudgy Brownie Overnight Oats

Orangey Vanilla with Toasted Coconut Overnight Oats

Peach Mango Streusel Overnight Oats

Maple Bacon Overnight Oats

Strawberry-Banana Baked Oatmeal Bars

Classic Chocolate Chip No-Bake Oatmeal Balls

Bacon Mushroom Melt Baked Oatmeal Bars

Blueberry Banana Oatmeal Muffins

Banana Oat Pancakes

Nutty Chocolate Chip Granola Bars

Chewy Peanut Butter Chocolate Chip Oatmeal Cookies

Chocolate Chip Oatmeal Bars

Conclusion

Introduction

Welcome! You've opened this book, and so I know you're serious about trying to start a healthy lifestyle. There's so much room for improvement, but the fact that you've decided to incorporate oatmeal into your diet is a huge leap that may lead to other progress in your journey to having a healthy lifestyle.

In this recipe book, I have decided to think out of the box. I wanted to recreate the drinks and desserts that I keep craving. I have tried and tested all 30 recipes over and over again, trying to incorporate whatever improvement I can, based on the constructive criticisms I have received from family and friends.

Now it's here. This book will help you prepare your oatmeal without worrying about failing it in the first try. Read through and try each recipe.

Oatmeal Recipes:

Peanut Butter and Raspberry Jelly Stovetop Oatmeal

Nothing beats waking up in a cold morning and eating a warm bowl of salty, sweet, and chunky oatmeal that will fill you up for a long time.

Prep Time: 15 minutes

Serving Size: 2 servings

Ingredients:

- 2 cups of milk of choice
- 1 cup rolled oats
- 3 tablespoons peanut butter
- 2 tablespoons raspberry jam (but any fruit jam or jelly of choice works too)
- 1/4 cup fresh raspberries
- 2 tablespoons roasted peanuts, chopped

Directions:

1. In a saucepan, heat the milk and bring to a boil.

2. In medium-high heat, add the oatmeal, peanut butter, and fruit jam to the mixture.

3. Stir for 7 minutes or more depending on your desired texture, or until the mixture starts to thicken.

4. Let it simmer and occasionally stir until all the liquid is absorbed.

5. Transfer oats to the bowls and top with fresh raspberries and nuts.

Spiced Pumpkin Stovetop Oatmeal with Pecans

Pumpkin spice is not only for lattes and pies. You can recreate your favorite drink or pie and incorporate it into your oatmeal. Even better, you can top it with pecans to complete the experience.

Prep Time: 12 minutes

Serving Size: 2 servings

Ingredients:

- 1 1/2 cups of milk of choice
- 1 cup rolled oats
- 2 tablespoons maple syrup or sweetener of choice
- 1/8 teaspoon ground nutmeg
- 1/8 teaspoon allspice
- 1/4 teaspoon ground ginger
- 1/2 teaspoon ground cinnamon
- 1/2 cup pumpkin puree
- 1/4 teaspoon salt

- 2 tablespoons pecans, chopped

Directions:

1. In a saucepan, boil the milk.

2. Lower the heat to medium-high, then add the rolled oats, sweetener, cinnamon, ginger, allspice, nutmeg, pumpkin puree, and salt.

3. Let it simmer while stirring occasionally for about 7 minutes or until the mixture thickens.

4. Transfer oats to the bowl/s and top with chopped pecans.

Cheesy Mushroom Stovetop Oatmeal

You might be used to eating your oatmeal sweet, but you should try this recipe when you want something new. This tastes savory with the right amount of spice to it.

Prep Time: 15 minutes

Serving Size: 2 servings

Ingredients:

- 1 tablespoon salted butter
- 1 cup button mushrooms, chopped
- 1 clove of garlic, minced
- 1 teaspoon dried thyme leaves
- Pinch of salt
- Pinch of pepper
- 1 cup spinach, chopped
- 2 cups vegetable broth

- 1 cup rolled oats
- 1/4 teaspoon red pepper flakes
- 1/4 cup cheese of choice (preferably mozzarella, cheddar, or goat cheese)

Directions:

1. In a saucepan, melt the butter.

2. Add the mushroom and let it cook for 5 minutes or until they become soft and it turns golden brown.

3. Add the garlic, thyme, salt, and pepper then toss for about 30 seconds.

4. Add the spinach and cook for another 2 minutes or until the leaves begin to wilt.

5. Pour the broth, oats, and red pepper flakes.

6. Bring the mixture into a simmer while occasionally stirring for about 6 minutes.

7. Once the liquid is absorbed fully, transfer to the bowls and top with cheese.

Cherry Chocolate Almond Stovetop Oatmeal

Satisfy your chocolate cravings all at once during breakfast to avoid added sugar intake. This recipe will satisfy your sweet tooth first thing in the morning and will keep you full until lunchtime.

Prep Time: 15 minutes

Serving Size: 2 servings

Ingredients:

- 2 cups of milk of choice
- 1 cup rolled oats
- 3 tablespoons maple syrup
- 1/2 cup cherries (fresh, frozen, dried, or canned), halved
- 1 tablespoon cocoa powder
- 3 tablespoons Greek yogurt

- 1/4 cup almonds, chopped

Directions:

1. In a saucepan, heat the milk and bring to a boil.

2. In medium-high heat, add the oats, maple syrup, cherries, and cocoa powder.

3. Let it simmer and stir for 7 minutes or more, depending on your desired texture, or until the mixture starts to thicken.

4. Transfer the oats to the bowl/s and top with yogurt and almonds.

Sriracha Soy Green Onions and Corn Stovetop Oatmeal

Again, another unlikely match which you might never have thought about, but you should try out if you want something savory and a bit of spiciness to your oats.

Prep Time: 15 minutes

Serving Size: 2 servings

Ingredients:

- 2 cups vegetable broth
- 1 cup rolled oats
- 2 tablespoons soy sauce
- Pinch of salt

- Pinch of pepper
- 1 teaspoon Sriracha
- 1 cup corn kernel (fresh, frozen, or canned)
- 1/2 cup green onions, chopped and divided
- 2 eggs

Directions:

1. Boil the vegetable broth in a medium pot.

2. Lower the heat to medium-high and add the oats, soy sauce, salt, pepper, and Sriracha in the broth.

3. Stir occasionally and let it simmer for about 7 minutes or until it begins to thicken.

4. Add the corn and 1/4 cup of green onions, then stir for another 2 minutes or until the corn gets cooked. Set aside.

5. Cook two sunny-side-up eggs, then set aside.

6. Transfer the oats to the bowls and top with the sunny-side-up eggs.

7. Garnish with the remaining green onions.

Copy-Cat Carrot Cake Stovetop Oatmeal

This recipe will not give you a real carrot cake, but it will make you a satisfying carrot cake alternative. The flavors will transform your oats into a whole new level. It's as if you are eating the cake itself.

Prep Time: 20 minutes

Serving Size: 2 servings

Ingredients:

- 2 cups of milk of choice
- 1 cup rolled oats
- 1 1/4 cups carrots, shredded and divided into 1 cup and 1/4 cup
- 1 teaspoon ground cinnamon
- 1/4 teaspoon ginger, minced
- 1/8 teaspoon ground nutmeg
- 2 tablespoons maple syrup
- 1 teaspoon vanilla extract
- 1/4 cup raisins
- 1/4 cup walnuts, chopped

Directions:

1. Boil the milk in a pot.

2. Lower the heat to medium-high and add the oats, a cup of carrots, cinnamon, ginger, nutmeg, maple syrup, and vanilla.

3. Let it simmer for about 7 minutes or until the mixture becomes thick and most of the liquid is absorbed while stirring it occasionally.

4. Add the raisins and walnuts then constantly stir for another minute.

5. Transfer oats to the bowls and top with the remaining carrots.

Creamy Coconut and Strawberry Stovetop Oatmeal

Here's a recipe to make your mornings even sweeter. Strawberries and cream always make a perfect pair when it comes to desserts or even drinks. So why not transform your oatmeal into one?

Prep Time: 20 minutes

Serving Size: 4 servings

Ingredients:

- 4 cups of milk of choice
- 2 cups rolled oats
- 2 cups of strawberries (fresh or frozen), chopped and divided into 1 1/2 cups and 1/2 cup
- 2 tablespoons chia seeds
- 1 medium banana, mashed
- 1 teaspoon vanilla extract

- 2 tablespoons maple syrup
- 4 tablespoons coconut cream

Directions:

1. In a medium pot, boil the milk.

2. Lower the heat to medium-high and add the oats, 1 1/2 cups of strawberries, chia seeds, banana, vanilla, and maple syrup.

3. Stir occasionally for 10 minutes or until the liquid is absorbed and the mixture thickens.

4. Transfer the oatmeal to the bowl/s and top with coconut cream and the remaining strawberries.

Nutty Cinnamon Blueberries and Peaches Stovetop Oatmeal

Blueberries and peaches are refreshing fruits that make this oatmeal recipe perfect for those who want a fruity bowl with the right amount of cinnamon and nut butter kick to it.

Prep Time: 10 minutes

Serving Size: 1 serving

Ingredients:

- 1 cup of water
- 1/2 cup rolled oats
- 1 tablespoon nut butter of choice
- 1 cup peaches (fresh or canned), chopped into bite-size pieces and divided
- 1/2 cup blueberries (fresh, frozen, or canned), divided
- 1/2 teaspoon vanilla extract
- 1/4 teaspoon ground cinnamon
- 1/2 tablespoon ground flaxseed

Directions:

1. In a saucepan, boil the water.

2. Lower the heat to medium-high and add the oats, nut butter, 1/2 cup of peaches, 1/4 cup of blueberries, vanilla, and cinnamon.

3. Let it simmer while occasionally stirring for 5 minutes until the liquid is absorbed or until the mixture thickens to the consistency you like.

4. Transfer to the bowl/s and top with the remaining peaches, blueberries, and flaxseed.

Creamy Mango Coconut Stovetop Oatmeal

Try this creamy mango coconut oatmeal recipe if you want that tropical taste first thing in the morning. The mangoes with coconut milk and cream are refreshing, and the coconut flakes give that crunch and chew to it.

Prep Time: 10 minutes

Serving Size: 2 servings

Ingredients:

- 2 cups of coconut milk
- Pinch of salt
- 1 cup rolled oats
- 2 tablespoons coconut flakes
- 4 tablespoons coconut cream
- 1/2 cup mangoes (fresh or frozen), chopped and divided

Directions:

1. In a saucepan, heat the milk until it boils.

2. Lower the heat to medium-high and add the salt and oats.

3. Allow the mixture to simmer for 7 minutes while stirring it occasionally.

4. Once the mixture thickens or it has reached your desired consistency, transfer to the bowls.

5. In a separate skillet, toast the coconut flakes for about 2 minutes or until it becomes golden brown.

6. Top the oatmeal bowls with coconut cream, mangoes, and coconut flakes.

Salted Caramel Apple Pie Stovetop Oatmeal

If you love apple pie so much just as I do, then this recipe is for you. The salted caramel complements the apple pie taste to it, making it a match made in heaven.

Prep Time: 17 minutes

Serving Size: 2 servings

Ingredients:

- 1 tablespoon butter
- 1 medium apple, diced
- 1 teaspoon ground cinnamon
- 2 cups of water or milk of choice
- Pinch of salt
- 1 cup rolled oats
- 1 tablespoon brown sugar
- Salted caramel sauce to drizzle

Directions:

1. In a skillet, melt the butter then add the apple and cinnamon.

2. Stir the mixture for about 6 minutes or until the apple becomes soft and turns golden brown, then set aside.

3. In a saucepan, boil the water or milk.

4. Lower the heat to medium-high, then add the salt and oats.

5. Stir the mixture occasionally for 5 to 7 minutes or until the liquid is absorbed, and it thickens up.

6. Add in the apple-cinnamon together with the brown sugar.

7. Stir for 30 seconds or until everything is incorporated.

8. Transfer to the bowl/s and drizzle with salted caramel sauce.

Cheesy Bacon Stovetop Oatmeal with Egg

This savory oatmeal recipe makes for breakfast or brunch. It is filling complete with eggs, cheese, and bacon. It's like your typical sandwich but in oatmeal form.

Prep Time: 20 minutes

Serving Size: 1 serving

Ingredients:

- 3 strips of bacon, chopped or minced depending on your preference
- 1 large egg
- 1 1/2 cups of water
- 3/4 cup rolled oats
- 1 scallion, chopped (separate the whites from the greens)
- 1 tablespoon butter
- 2 teaspoons salt, divided
- 1 teaspoon ground black pepper

- 2 tablespoons heavy cream
- 2 tablespoons cheddar cheese, shredded

Directions:

1. In a non-stick pan, sauté the chopped bacon until it becomes crispy, then set the bacon aside, leaving the oil of the bacon.

2. Using the same pan, cook a sunny-side-up egg, and set aside.

3. In a saucepan, boil the water together with the whites of the scallion, butter, and a teaspoon of salt.

4. Lower the heat to medium-high and add the oats.

5. Let it simmer while occasionally stirring for 7 minutes or until the liquid is absorbed and mixture thickens.

6. Transfer oatmeal to a bowl.

7. Heat the heavy cream and pour the warm cream on top of the oatmeal.

8. Top the bowl with the egg, shredded cheese, bacon, and the greens of the scallion.

Creamy Coconut Cafe Latte Overnight Oatmeal

The bitter taste of the coffee complements the coconut milk and cream so well to satisfy the coffee lover in you. It won't be enough for your early morning coffee fix, but it will be a good introduction to your day.

Prep Time: 2 hours and 5 minutes

Serving Size: 2 servings

Ingredients:

- 1 cup rolled oats
- 1/4 cup freshly brewed coffee or cold brew
- 3/4 cup coconut milk
- 2 tablespoons maple syrup or sweetener of choice
- 1 teaspoon ground cinnamon, divided

- 1/4 cup coconut cream
- 1/4 cup coconut flakes or chips

Directions:

1. In a container, place the oats, coffee, coconut milk, sweetener, and half a teaspoon of cinnamon.

2. Mix the ingredients well and make sure that everything is well-incorporated.

3. Cover the container.

4. Place it in the refrigerator for at least 2 hours, but preferably overnight.

5. Before serving, top with the coconut cream, coconut flakes, and the remaining cinnamon.

Birthday Cake Overnight Oats

Birthday cake is something that brings out the inner child in us. Not only does it look pleasing to the eyes, but it can satisfy our sweet cravings. Give your oatmeal the transformation it deserves, complete with rainbow sprinkles.

Prep Time: 2 hours and 5 minutes

Serving Size: 2 servings

Ingredients:

- 1/2 cup Greek yogurt
- 1 tablespoon chia seeds
- 1 cup rolled oats
- 1 cup of milk of choice

- 1 tablespoon of honey or sweetener of choice
- 1 tablespoon rainbow sprinkles
- 2 teaspoons vanilla extract

Directions:

1. Place all the ingredients in a container except for the rainbow sprinkles.

2. Give the mixture a good stir to make sure that everything is well-incorporated.

3. Cover the container.

4. Place it in the fridge for at least 2 hours or leave it there overnight.

5. Transfer the oatmeal in the bowl/s then drizzle the rainbow sprinkles.

Strawberry Cheesecake-Inspired Overnight Oatmeal

Why limit cheesecakes for desserts when you can have it for breakfast? We don't put in actual cream cheese in this recipe, but the Greek yogurt does the trick to give it a tangy taste that you always look for in cheesecakes.

Prep Time: 2 hours and 10 minutes

Serving Size: 2 servings

Ingredients:

- 1 cup strawberries (fresh or frozen)
- 3/4 cup of milk of choice
- 1/2 cup Greek yogurt
- 1 cup rolled oats
- 1 tablespoon chia seeds
- Pinch of salt
- 1 tablespoon honey or sweetener of choice
- 1 teaspoon vanilla extract
- 2 tablespoons of graham crackers, crushed
- 2 tablespoons of strawberry jam

Directions:

1. Make a puree by blending in a food processor or regular blender the strawberries, milk, and yogurt.

2. In a container, mix the puree with the oats, chia seeds, salt, sweetener, and vanilla.

3. Cover the container.

4. Place it in the refrigerator for at least 2 hours or leave it there overnight.

5. Transfer the oatmeal to the bowl/s and drizzle with strawberry jam and crushed graham.

Blueberry Overnight Oats

Blueberries are always a crowd-favorite to pair with oatmeal. However, this recipe is more than that. It tastes tangy, crunchy, and creamy, all at once.

Prep Time: 2 hours and 10 minutes

Serving Size: 2 servings

Ingredients:

- 3/4 cup blueberries (fresh or frozen, but fresh is best for this recipe), divided into 1/2 cup and 1/4 cup
- 3/4 cup milk of choice
- 1 teaspoon vanilla extract
- 1 cup rolled oats
- 2 tablespoons chia seeds
- 1 1/2 teaspoon lemon zest, divided into 1 teaspoon and 1/2 teaspoon
- pinch of salt
- 4 tablespoons trail mix or granola

- 1/2 cup Greek yogurt

Directions:

1. In a bowl, mash 1/2 cup of blueberries using a fork.

2. Add the yogurt, milk, and vanilla, then stir well.

3. Add the oats, chia seeds, a teaspoon of lemon zest, and salt, then stir well.

4. Transfer to a container, then cover it.

5. Refrigerate the oats for at least 2 hours, but preferably overnight.

6. Once ready to serve, transfer to the bowl/s, then top with trail mix or granola and the remaining blueberries and lemon zest.

French Toast-Flavored Overnight Oats

If you want to have a French toast, but only have oatmeal at home, then this recipe is perfect to curb your craving. It's simple to make and satisfyingly sweet and delicious.

Prep Time: 2 hours and 5 minutes

Serving Size: 2 servings

Ingredients:

- 1 banana, divided
- 1 cup rolled oats
- 1 teaspoon ground cinnamon, divided
- 1/2 teaspoon vanilla extract
- 1 tablespoon maple syrup
- 1 teaspoon flaxseed meal
- 1 cup of milk of choice
- 1/2 cup mixed berries (fresh or frozen, but fresh is best for toppings)

Directions:

1. Mash half of the banana in a bowl.

2. Add the oats, half a teaspoon of cinnamon, vanilla, maple syrup, flaxseed meal, and milk, then mix well.

3. Transfer to a container, then cover it.

4. Place in the fridge for at least 2 hours or overnight.

5. For the toppings, slice the remaining banana and the mixed berries into bite-sized pieces.

6. Finish off with a drizzle of the remaining cinnamon.

Coco-Mango and Ginger Overnight Oats

This overnight oats recipe has the right balance of creamy and fruity taste to it. The coconut cream and mango each have their distinct flavor while complementing the ginger's taste.

Prep Time: 2 hours and 10 minutes

Serving Size: 4 servings

Ingredients:

- 2 cups rolled oats
- 1 1/3 cups of water
- 2/3 cup of coconut milk
- 2 tablespoons honey or any sweetener of choice
- 1/2 teaspoon fresh ginger, shredded
- 1/2 cup coconut cream

- 2 cups mango (fresh or frozen), cubed

Directions:

1. In a bowl, mix the oats, water, milk, sweetener, and ginger, then give it a good stir to ensure that everything is mixed and that the oats are soaked well.

2. Transfer to a container, then cover it.

3. Store in the refrigerator for at least 2 hours or overnight.

4. Before serving, pour coconut cream and top with mangoes.

Blueberry Muffin-Tasting Overnight Oats

If you want blueberry muffins, but don't have an oven, you can try the other ways, such as making overnight oats that closely resembles the taste of blueberry muffins.

Prep Time: 2 hours and 5 minutes

Serving Size: 1 serving

Ingredients:

- 1/2 cup blueberries (fresh or frozen), divided
- 1/4 cup Greek yogurt
- 1/2 cup rolled oats
- 1/2 cup of milk of choice
- 1/2 teaspoon vanilla extract
- 1 tablespoon vanilla pudding mix
- 1/3 cup cereal of choice
- 1 teaspoon ground cinnamon

Directions:

1. Blend the 1/4 cup of blueberries with the yogurt, then pour the mixture into a bowl.

2. Add the oats, milk, vanilla extract, and pudding mix, then stir well. See to it that the oats are soaked well.

3. Transfer to a container, then cover it.

4. Refrigerate for at least 2 hours or overnight.

5. When ready to serve, top with cereals and drizzle with cinnamon.

Fudgy Brownie Overnight Oats

Brownies will always have a space in our hearts and tummies. So, when I had the chance to recreate something that I loved, I did not hesitate. This oatmeal tastes just like your usual fudgy brownie, that's why you should try this recipe.

Prep Time: 2 hours and 10 minutes

Serving Size: 1 serving

Ingredients:

- 1 tablespoon nut butter of choice
- 1/3 cup Greek yogurt
- 2/3 cup chocolate milk of choice
- 1/2 cup rolled oats
- 2 tablespoons Dutch-processed cocoa powder

- 1/2 teaspoon vanilla extract
- A pinch of salt
- 1 tablespoon maple syrup or sweetener of choice
- 1 tablespoon semi-sweet chocolate chips

Directions:

1. In a bowl, mix the nut butter, yogurt, milk, oats, cocoa powder, vanilla, salt, and sweetener thoroughly.

2. Taste test the mixture. If you prefer it to be sweeter, then add some more sweetener.

3. Transfer to a container, then cover it.

4. Place in the refrigerator for at least 2 hours or overnight.

5. Once ready, top the oatmeal with chocolate chips.

Orangey Vanilla with Toasted Coconut Overnight Oats

Vanilla tastes as good as always. But when you add orange juice and zest, it tastes even better. Plus, the toasted desiccated coconut gives it a burnt taste that tops it all.

Prep Time: 2 hours and 5 minutes

Serving Size: 4 servings

Ingredients:

- 2 tablespoons desiccated coconut
- 2 cups rolled oats
- 1 1/2 cups of milk of choice

- 1/2 cup Greek yogurt
- 1/2 cup fresh orange juice
- 1 teaspoon vanilla extract
- 1 tablespoon orange zest, divided

Directions:

1. In a skillet, toast the desiccated coconut over medium-high heat until it turns golden brown then set aside. This step is optional. You can mix the desiccated coconut as is without toasting it.

2. In a bowl, mix the oats, milk, yogurt, orange juice, a tablespoon of desiccated coconut, vanilla, and half a tablespoon of orange zest.

3. Transfer to a container, then cover it.

4. Store in the refrigerator for at least 2 hours or overnight.

5. Transfer to the bowl/s and serve topped with the remaining desiccated coconut and orange zest.

Peach Mango Streusel Overnight Oats

This dessert-ish breakfast is just like your usual streusel but topped on your overnight oats. It's sweet and goes well with the oats to balance out its sweetness.

Prep Time: 2 hours and 8 minutes

Serving Size: 1 serving

Ingredients:

- 1/2 cup + 1 tablespoon rolled oats, divided
- 2/3 cup of milk of choice
- 1/3 cup Greek yogurt
- 1 1/2 tablespoons maple syrup or any sweetener of choice
- 1 teaspoon vanilla extract, divided
- 1/2 teaspoon ground cinnamon, divided

- 1/8 teaspoon salt
- 1/4 cup peaches (fresh or canned), cubed
- 1/4 cup ripe mangoes (fresh or frozen, but fresh works best for this recipe), cubed
- 1 tablespoon coconut oil, divided
- 1/2 tablespoon white flour
- 1/2 tablespoon brown sugar

Directions:

1. In a bowl, mix thoroughly half a cup of maple syrup, oats, yogurt, milk, half a teaspoon of vanilla, a quarter teaspoon of cinnamon, and salt.

2. Transfer to a container, then cover it.

3. Store in the fridge for at least 2 hours or overnight.

4. When you're ready to eat, in a skillet, heat the peaches and mangoes together with half a tablespoon of coconut oil, and the remaining vanilla, over medium-low heat for 2 minutes or until the mixture becomes fragrant. Set aside.

5. To make the streusel, use the same skillet and melt the remaining coconut oil over medium-low heat.

6. Add the remaining rolled oats and cinnamon, white flour, and brown sugar.

7. Mix for about 2 minutes or until the oats turn golden brown and become crispy.

8. Once ready to serve, top the oatmeal with the peach, mango, and streusel.

Maple Bacon Overnight Oats

This combination of oatmeal, maple, and bacon will satisfy your taste bud for 100%.

Prep Time: 2 hours and 8 minutes

Serving Size: 2 servings

Ingredients:

- 1 cup rolled oats
- 1 cup of milk of choice
- 2 tablespoons walnuts, chopped
- 3 tablespoons maple syrup, divided into 1 tablespoon and 2 tablespoons
- 1/8 teaspoon ground cinnamon
- 4 strips of maple bacon

Directions:

1. In a bowl, mix thoroughly the oatmeal, milk, walnuts, a tablespoon of

maple syrup, and cinnamon until the oats are fully soaked.

2. Transfer to a container, then cover it.

3. Store in the refrigerator for at least 2 hours or overnight.

4. Before serving the oatmeal, in a skillet, cook the bacon until it becomes extra crispy.

5. Chop the bacon into tidbits then top on the oats with the remaining maple syrup.

Strawberry-Banana Baked Oatmeal Bars

Oatmeal is such a versatile ingredient. In this recipe, we are baking the oats with fresh strawberries, bananas, and chocolate chips. It's a sweet treat with loads of fiber for you to snack on.

Prep Time: 1 hour and 10 minutes

Serving Size: 6 bars

Ingredients:

- cooking oil to grease the baking pan
- 2 cups rolled oats
- 1 teaspoon baking powder
- 1 teaspoon ground cinnamon
- 1/2 teaspoon of salt
- 2 cups of milk of choice
- 1/4 cup maple syrup
- 1 large egg
- 2 tablespoons coconut oil

- 2 teaspoons vanilla extract
- 2 ripe bananas, divided (one mashed, the other sliced)
- 1 1/2 cups fresh strawberries, quartered and divided into 1 cup and 1/2 cup
- 1/4 cup semi-sweet chocolate chips, divided

Directions:

1. Pre-heat your oven at 375 degrees Fahrenheit.

2. Brush an 8x8 baking pan with oil.

3. In a bowl, add the oats, cinnamon, baking powder, and salt then mix well.

4. Add the milk, maple syrup, egg, coconut oil, vanilla, and mashed banana, then stir thoroughly.

5. Incorporate a cup of strawberries by folding it with a spatula, followed by half of the sliced banana, and an eighth cup of the chocolate chips.

6. Transfer the mixture into the baking pan.

7. Top with the remaining strawberries, banana, and chocolate chips.

8. Bake in the oven for 50 to 60 minutes or until the sides become golden. You might notice that the middle portion is quite wet, but this will begin to dry up once we leave it to cool.

9. Remove from the oven and allow it to cool for 10 to 15 minutes before slicing.

Classic Chocolate Chip No-Bake Oatmeal Balls

No oven, no problem! When you are looking for the healthy oatmeal hacks for snacks, these no-bake oatmeal balls are perfect for you. It's like chocolate chip cookie dough, but with rolled oats instead of your usual all-purpose flour.

Prep Time: 40 minutes

Serving Size: 18 balls

Ingredients:

- 1 1/4 cups rolled oats
- 1/2 cup nut butter of choice
- 1/3 cup honey or any sticky sweetener of choice
- 1/4 teaspoon salt
- 2 tablespoons chia seeds
- 1/2 cup semi-sweet chocolate chips

Directions:

1. In a mixing bowl, place all the ingredients and stir to ensure that all the ingredients are combined well.

2. Depending on your preference, you can add more oats if you find the mixture to be too wet. If you find it too dry, then add more nut butter to add moisture.

3. You would know that it has the right consistency when the dough batter can hold on its own when rolled into balls.

4. To make it easier to work with the dough, you can leave it in the fridge to chill for 30 minutes then roll them into balls.

Bacon Mushroom Melt Baked Oatmeal Bars

If you need a break from all the sweet oatmeal pairings, then this savory baked oatmeal recipe will cut it. Bacon, mushroom, and cheese are the usual add-ons to burgers, but since oatmeal is life, I decided to give it a remake with some caramelized onions.

Prep Time: 1 hour

Serving Size: 6 bars

Ingredients:

- 1 tablespoon extra-virgin olive oil
- 4 cups yellow onions, sliced into half-moon shapes
- 1/2 teaspoon salt
- 4 cups of water, divided into 2 cups each
- 3 strips of thick smoked bacon
- 3 cups shiitake mushrooms, sliced
- 1 cup rolled oats
- Cooking oil to grease the baking pan

- 2 tablespoons fresh parsley, chopped
- 1/4 teaspoon pepper

Directions:

1. In a skillet, caramelize onions by heating the olive oil in medium-low heat.

2. Add a pinch of salt and the onions, then stir continuously.

3. Pour a quarter cup of water in the mixture and keep stirring.

4. Observe and wait for the onions to begin to brown and caramelize.

5. It will take about 20 minutes for the onions to have a bittersweet taste.

6. To avoid the onions from sticking and getting burnt, add another quarter cup or a sufficient amount of water every time the water evaporates.

7. Once the onions have caramelized, set it aside.

8. Using the same skillet, cook the bacon until it becomes extra crispy.

9. Remove the bacon and set it aside but leave the oil to cook the shiitake mushrooms for about 3 to 5 minutes.

10. Chop the bacon strips into tidbits.

11. Preheat the oven to 450 degrees Fahrenheit.

12. In a saucepan, boil 2 cups of water.

13. Add the oats and let it simmer while stirring continuously until the liquid is absorbed.

14. Brush a 12-inch baking pan with oil.

15. In a bowl, add the cooked oats, bacon, mushrooms, caramelized onions, parsley, salt, and pepper.

16. Combine all the ingredients then pour into the greased baking pan.

17. Bake for 10 to 12 minutes or until the top turns light brown.

Blueberry Banana Oatmeal Muffins

I guarantee that these Blueberry Banana Oatmeal Muffins will become your and your family's favorite after just one bite!

Prep Time: 35 minutes

Serving Size: 12 muffins

Ingredients:

- 1 large banana, sliced into small cubes
- 1 cup blueberries
- zest of 1/2 of a lemon
- 1/4 cup vegetable oil
- 1 egg, lightly beaten
- 1/2 cup brown sugar, packed
- 1/2 teaspoon salt
- 1/2 teaspoon baking soda
- 1 teaspoon baking powder
- 1 cup of all-purpose flour
- 1 cup buttermilk
- 1 cup rolled oats

Directions:

1. Preheat the oven to 400 degrees Fahrenheit.

2. Line the muffin cups with paper.

3. In a small bowl, add the oats and buttermilk then combine until the oats become soaked. Set aside.

4. In another bowl, whisk the dry ingredients - flour, baking powder, baking soda, salt, and brown sugar. Set aside.

5. In the oatmeal mixture bowl, add the egg, oil, and lemon zest. Mix until everything is well-combined.

6. Add the pre-mixed dry ingredients to the oatmeal mixture bowl and stir until the dry ingredients are fully incorporated with the wet ingredients.

7. Fold the blueberries and banana cubes in the mixture.

8. Transfer the batter into the muffin cups filling only 3/4 of the cup.

9. Bake for 15 to 22 minutes.

10. Remove from the oven.

11. Let it cool for another 5 minutes.

Banana Oat Pancakes

The base of this pancake batter is oatmeal, banana, and eggs. These three ingredients make a good batter without the need for flour, plus the sweetness in the banana will require lesser sugar.

Prep Time: 20 minutes

Serving Size: 10 pancakes

Ingredients:

- 1/2 cup of milk of choice
- 2 eggs
- 1 egg white
- 1 banana
- 2 tablespoons maple syrup or any sweetener of choice
- 1 teaspoon vanilla extract

- 1 1/2 cups rolled oats
- 2 teaspoons baking powder
- 1/2 teaspoon salt

Directions:

1. In a food processor, blend all the ingredients until the mixture becomes smooth and thick like the usual pancake batter.

2. Heat a non-stick pan.

3. Over medium-low heat, pour the pancake batter by batches and cook for 2 to 3 minutes on one side.

4. Flip it over and cook for another minute or 2, then remove.

Nutty Chocolate Chip Granola Bars

This recipe is a basic granola bar made with oats, nut butter, honey, nuts, and chocolate chips. It's simple, so there's no excuse for beginners not to try it.

Prep Time: 1 hour and 5 minutes

Serving Size: 8 servings

Ingredients:

- 1 cup nut butter of choice (choose one that has a smooth consistency as this will be one of the binders for the rest of the ingredients)
- 2/3 cup honey
- 1 teaspoon vanilla extract
- 1/2 teaspoon salt
- 2 1/2 cups rolled oats
- 1/2 cup semi-sweet chocolate chips
- 3 tablespoons cashew nuts or any nut of choice, chopped

Directions:

1. Using a parchment paper, line an 8x8 baking pan.

2. In a bowl, add the nut butter, honey, vanilla, and salt, then stir until the mixture has a smooth consistency.

3. Add the oats, chocolate chips, and nuts into the bowl and mix until everything is well-combined.

4. It is time to transfer to the baking pan when the oats, chips, and nuts come together when you take a scoop of it.

5. Once the mixture is in the pan, layer with another parchment paper and flatten it using a bowl or anything with a flat surface.

6. Chill in the fridge for at least 1 hour before slicing and serving.

Chewy Peanut Butter Chocolate Chip Oatmeal Cookies

Oatmeal cookies are one of the classic cookies that a lot of people love. So, I decided to take it up a notch by making chewy oatmeal cookies with peanut butter and chocolate chips.

Prep Time: 1 hour and 10 minutes

Serving Size: 32 cookies

Ingredients:

- 1 teaspoon baking powder
- 1 ½ cups of all-purpose flour
- 1 teaspoon baking soda
- 2 cups rolled oats
- 1 cup butter, softened
- 1 cup brown sugar, packed
- 1/2 cup white sugar
- 1 1/2 cups all-purpose flour
- 1 cup of creamy peanut butter

- 2 teaspoons vanilla extract
- 2 1/2 cups semi-sweet chocolate chips
- 2 large eggs

Directions:

1. In a bowl, add the flour, baking powder, baking soda, and salt, then whisk until everything is combined. Set aside.

2. In another bowl, cream the butter with the brown and white sugar using a hand mixer for about 3 minutes on medium-high speed.

3. Add the eggs, peanut butter, and vanilla.

4. Beat the mixture using a hand mixer for another minute on high speed.

5. Add the pre-mixed dry ingredients to the wet ingredients, by folding it gently using a spatula.

6. Fold in the oats.

7. Fold in the chocolate chips.

8. Chill the cookie dough for about 20 minutes.

9. Preheat oven to 350 degrees Fahrenheit.

10. Line baking sheets using parchment paper then set aside.

11. Scoop about two tablespoons of dough and roll them into a ball.

12. Keep a 3-inch distance between each ball.

13. Bake for 12 to 14 minutes or until you see the sides begin to turn light brown.

14. Remove from the oven.

15. Let it cool for about 5 minutes, then transfer to a wire rack.

Chocolate Chip Oatmeal Bars

Cookies are great, but bars make for softer and moister treats. If you're bored with eating cookies, make yourself some homemade bars, and you'll love this classic recipe.

Prep Time: 1 hour

Serving Size: 12 bars

Ingredients:

- 1 cup butter, softened
- 2/3 cup brown sugar, packed
- 2/3 cup white sugar
- 2 eggs
- 2 teaspoons vanilla extract

- 1 cup of all-purpose flour
- 1 teaspoon baking powder
- 1/2 teaspoon salt
- 2 cups rolled oats
- 1 1/4 cups chocolate chips, divided

Directions:

1. Preheat oven to 350 degrees Fahrenheit.

2. Line a 9x12 baking pan with parchment paper then set aside.

3. Cream the butter with the white and brown sugar using an electric mixer over medium-high speed for about 3 minutes.

4. Add the eggs and vanilla, then beat with an electric mixer over medium-high speed until the mixture becomes fluffy.

5. Gently fold the flour, baking powder, salt, oats, and a cup of chocolate chips in the wet ingredients.

6. Pour the batter in the baking pan.

7. Top with the remaining chocolate chips.

8. Bake for about 40 minutes or until you can see the sides pulling away from the pan.

9. Remove from the oven.

10. Let it cool for another 5 to 10 minutes before slicing.

www.ingramcontent.com/pod-product-compliance
Lightning Source LLC
Chambersburg PA
CBHW030820090125
20114CB00024B/420